Copyright © 2023 by Michael Jaynes (Author)

This book is protected by copyright law and is intended solely for personal use. Reproduction, distribution, or any other form of use requires the written permission of the author. The information presented in this book is for educational and entertainment purposes only, and while every effort has been made to ensure its accuracy and completeness, no guarantees are made. The author is not providing legal, financial, medical, or professional advice, and readers should consult with a licensed professional before implementing any of the techniques discussed in this book. The content in this book has been sourced from various reliable sources, but readers should exercise their own judgment when using this information. The author is not responsible for any losses, direct or indirect, that may occur from the use of this book, including but not limited to errors, omissions, or inaccuracies.

We hope this book has been informative and helpful on your journey to understanding and celebrating older adults. Thank you for your interest and support!

Title: The Roots of the Score Sheet-Uncovering the Early Years of Football's Best Goal Makers
Subtitle: The Deadliest Finishers in the History of Football

Series: Striking Gold: Top Scorers in Football before the 1980s
By Michael Jaynes

"Football is a simple game. Twenty-two men chase a ball for 90 minutes and at the end, the Germans always win."
Gary Lineker

"Some people think football is a matter of life and death. I assure you, it's much more serious than that."
Bill Shankly

"Football was different back then. It was more about the love of the game and the joy of scoring goals than it was about money and fame."
Pele

"The early days of football were a magical time. There was a purity to the sport that has been lost in modern times."
Bobby Charlton

"The great goal scorers of the past were true artists. They had a sense of poetry and beauty that is rarely seen in the game today."
Eusebio

"The goal scorers of the past were not just great athletes, they were also great storytellers. They could create drama and tension with every shot they took."
Nándor Hidegkuti

"The ball is round, the game lasts 90 minutes, and everything else is just theory."
Josef Herberger

Table of Contents

Introduction 7
Overview of the book 7
Historical context of football and its evolution 9
Importance of goal scorers in football 11

Chapter 1: Josef Bican - Czechoslovakia - 657 goals (545 club + 112 national) - retired 1955 13
Early life and football career beginnings 13
Rise to fame as a prolific goal scorer 16
Key achievements and records 18
Legacy and impact on football 20

Chapter 2: Eusebio - Portugal - 621 goals (473 club + 148 national) - retired 1979 23
Childhood and early football career 23
Success with Benfica and national team 26
Performance at the 1966 World Cup 29
Legacy and impact on Portuguese football 31

Chapter 3: Leônidas - Brazil - 358 goals (344 club + 14 national) - retired 1942 34
Early life and rise to fame 34
Success with Flamengo and the Brazilian national team 37
Performance at the 1938 World Cup 40
Legacy and impact on Brazilian football 42

Chapter 4: Gyula Zsengellér - Hungary - 354 goals (338 club + 16 national) - retired 1942 45
Early life and football career beginnings 45

5

Rise to fame as a goal scorer in Hungary and Austria............ 48

Success with the Hungarian national team............................... 52

Legacy and impact on Hungarian football 54

Chapter 5: Sándor Kocsis - Hungary - 331 goals (257 club + 74 national) - retired 1961 56

Childhood and early football career.. 56

Success with Honved and the Hungarian national team 58

Performance at the 1954 World Cup 60

Legacy and impact on Hungarian football 62

Chapter 6: Jimmy Greaves - England - 297 goals (268 club + 29 national) - retired 1971 64

Early life and rise to fame at Chelsea.. 64

Success with Tottenham and the English national team........... 66

Controversy and struggles later in his career 68

Legacy and impact on English football 70

Conclusion 73

Recap of the book's content... 73

Significance of goal scorers in football history 76

Future of goal scoring and its impact on the sport................... 78

Key Terms and Definitions 81

Supporting Materials... 83

Introduction
Overview of the book

Football is one of the most popular sports in the world, with millions of fans across the globe. At the heart of every football match is the goal, and the players who score them are celebrated as heroes. In this book, we take a unique and in-depth look at the early years of some of the greatest goal scorers in football history. From Josef Bican to Jimmy Greaves, we examine their humble beginnings and follow their rise to fame.

The Roots of the Score Sheet: Uncovering the Early Years of Football's Best Goal Makers is a comprehensive study of the roots of goal scoring. In this book, we aim to provide readers with a deeper understanding of what it takes to become a prolific goal scorer. We will explore the personal struggles, key achievements, and notable records of each player, as well as their legacy and impact on football.

This book is not just for die-hard fans of the game. It's also for anyone who enjoys reading about inspiring journeys. The stories of these players are about more than just football. They're about perseverance, dedication, and the pursuit of excellence.

The book is structured in six chapters, each focusing on a different goal scorer. We start with Josef Bican, who scored an incredible 657 goals during his career. From there, we move on to Eusebio, Leônidas, Gyula Zsengellér, Sándor Kocsis, and Jimmy Greaves. By examining players from different countries and eras, we hope to provide readers with a comprehensive look at the roots of goal scoring.

The book's conclusion will summarize the content covered in each chapter and highlight the significance of goal scorers in football history. We will also discuss the future of goal scoring and its impact on the sport.

Whether you're a football fan or simply interested in learning about inspiring stories, The Roots of the Score Sheet: Uncovering the Early Years of Football's Best Goal Makers is sure to captivate and inspire. Join us as we dive into the lives of some of the greatest goal scorers in football history and uncover the roots of their success.

Historical context of football and its evolution

To understand the roots of goal scoring in football, it's important to examine the historical context of the sport and how it has evolved over time. Football has a rich and complex history, with roots dating back centuries. In this section, we will explore the origins of football, its evolution, and how the sport has become the global phenomenon that it is today.

Origins of football:

The earliest forms of football can be traced back to ancient civilizations, such as China and Greece. These early games were often played using balls made of leather or animal bladders, and involved kicking the ball into a target or goal. Over time, different variations of football developed across Europe, with each country and region developing its own unique style of play.

Evolution of football:

The modern game of football as we know it today began to take shape in the 19th century, primarily in England. The first football clubs were established during this time, and the first official football match was played in 1863. Rules were standardized and codified, and the first football associations were established.

Over the years, football continued to evolve, with new tactics, strategies, and styles of play emerging. The game became more organized, with leagues and tournaments being established at the local, national, and international levels. Innovations such as the introduction of the offside rule, the use of goal nets, and the development of the penalty kick all contributed to the evolution of the sport.

Globalization of football:

The 20th century saw football become a truly global sport, with the establishment of international tournaments such as the World Cup and the Olympic Games. Football became a cultural phenomenon, with millions of fans across the world following their favorite teams and players. The sport became a symbol of national pride and identity, with each country developing its own unique football culture.

Conclusion:

The historical context of football and its evolution provide important background information for understanding the roots of goal scoring in the sport. Football has come a long way from its origins in ancient civilizations, and its evolution has been shaped by factors such as cultural, social, and economic influences. By examining the history of football, we can gain a deeper appreciation for the sport and how it has become a global phenomenon.

Importance of goal scorers in football

Football is a sport that has been played for centuries and has evolved significantly over time. One aspect of the game that has remained constant is the importance of scoring goals. Goals are what ultimately determine the outcome of a match, and as such, the role of the goal scorer is crucial. In this section, we will explore the importance of goal scorers in football and the impact they have on the game.

The role of the goal scorer is to put the ball into the back of the net, and in doing so, give their team an advantage. It is a skill that is highly valued in the sport, and for good reason. Goals are the most tangible and visible form of success in football, and as such, the goal scorer is often the most celebrated player on the pitch. They are the ones who make headlines, who are remembered long after their careers have ended, and who inspire future generations of footballers.

But the importance of goal scorers goes beyond just their ability to put the ball in the back of the net. They are often the players who provide the most excitement and entertainment for fans. A well-placed shot, a stunning header, or a perfectly executed free-kick can send a crowd into raptures, and it is the goal scorer who is responsible for creating these moments of magic.

The impact of a prolific goal scorer on a team cannot be overstated. They are the ones who can turn a match on its head with a single strike, who can lift their teammates and inspire them to greater heights, and who can strike fear into the hearts of opposition defenders. The presence of a top-class goal scorer can often be the difference between a successful season and a disappointing one, and as such, they are highly sought after by clubs around the world.

The importance of goal scorers in football is not just limited to the professional game. It is a skill that is highly valued at all levels of the sport, from grassroots to the highest levels of international competition. Young players are often encouraged to develop their goal-scoring ability, as it is seen as a key component of success in the game.

In conclusion, the role of the goal scorer in football is vital, and their impact on the game cannot be overstated. They are the ones who provide the excitement, the entertainment, and the moments of magic that make football such a beloved sport. Whether playing at the highest levels of the professional game or on a Sunday morning with friends, the importance of goal scorers remains constant. It is a skill that is highly valued and celebrated, and one that will continue to be a key component of the sport for generations to come.

Chapter 1: Josef Bican - Czechoslovakia - 657 goals (545 club + 112 national) - retired 1955

Early life and football career beginnings

Josef Bican was born on September 25, 1913, in Vienna, Austria-Hungary, to a Czech father and an Austrian mother. His father was a shoemaker, and Bican was the third of six children. His family lived in a working-class neighborhood, and Bican started playing football at a young age on the streets and parks near his home.

Bican's talent as a footballer was evident early on, and he quickly caught the attention of local clubs. He joined Hertha Vienna in 1928 at the age of 15 and played for their youth team before making his debut for the first team in 1931. Bican was a versatile player, capable of playing as a forward, midfielder, or defender, and he quickly established himself as a key player for Hertha Vienna.

In 1933, Bican joined Rapid Vienna, one of the most successful clubs in Austria at the time. It was at Rapid Vienna that Bican began to develop his reputation as a prolific goal scorer. In his first season with the club, Bican scored 27 goals in 21 matches, a remarkable feat for a player who was still relatively unknown.

Bican's performances at Rapid Vienna soon caught the attention of the Czechoslovakian national team, and he made his international debut in 1934. He scored a hat-trick in his second international match, and his performances for the national team helped Czechoslovakia win the 1934 Central European International Cup.

Bican's career was interrupted by the outbreak of World War II, during which he served in the Czechoslovakian army. However, he continued to play football during the war, and his performances for his military team caught the attention of Slavia Prague, one of the most successful clubs in Czechoslovakia.

Bican joined Slavia Prague in 1948 and helped the club win the Czechoslovakian league title in his first season. He continued to play for Slavia Prague until his retirement in 1955, at the age of 42.

Throughout his career, Bican was known for his speed, agility, and clinical finishing. He was a master of the dribble and was capable of scoring goals from almost any position on the pitch. Bican was also a pioneer of modern football tactics, and his ability to play in multiple positions made him a valuable asset for any team he played for.

Despite his success on the pitch, Bican's personal life was marked by tragedy. He lost his first wife and child in a bombing raid during World War II, and he later remarried and had three children with his second wife. Bican died on

December 12, 2001, in Prague, Czech Republic, at the age of 88.

In summary, Josef Bican's early life and football career beginnings were marked by his talent, versatility, and incredible goal-scoring ability. He rose from humble beginnings to become one of the most successful and respected players of his generation, and his legacy continues to inspire and influence footballers around the world.

Rise to fame as a prolific goal scorer

Josef Bican's rise to fame as a prolific goal scorer is a story of determination, hard work, and natural talent. He was a striker who was able to score goals with both his left and right feet, and he was also a very fast runner. Bican's skillset was unique, and it helped him rise to fame as one of the greatest goal scorers in football history.

Bican's prolific goal-scoring career started in the late 1920s when he was playing for Hertha Vienna. In his first season, he scored 27 goals in just 19 games, which was a remarkable achievement for a 17-year-old. Bican's pace and agility on the pitch made him almost unstoppable, and it was not long before he caught the attention of bigger clubs.

In 1931, Bican was signed by Rapid Vienna, where he spent the next six years of his career. It was during this period that he really established himself as one of the most prolific goal scorers in football history. In his first season with the club, he scored 44 goals in 24 games, which is still a record in Austrian football. He went on to score a total of 395 goals in just 217 appearances for Rapid Vienna, which remains a club record to this day.

Bican's success at Rapid Vienna did not go unnoticed, and in 1938 he was signed by Slavia Prague, one of the biggest clubs in Czechoslovakia at the time. Bican's time at

Slavia Prague was short, but he still managed to score an impressive 57 goals in just 26 games. He then moved to FC Vienna, where he continued to score goals at an incredible rate.

Bican's most remarkable achievement as a goal scorer came during the 1947-48 season when he scored an incredible 76 goals in just 42 games for Rapid Vienna. This was a record-breaking achievement, and it cemented Bican's place in football history as one of the greatest goal scorers of all time.

Despite his incredible goal-scoring record, Bican was also a team player. He was known for his unselfish play and his ability to create goals for his teammates. Bican was a hard worker both on and off the pitch, and his dedication to the game earned him the respect of players, coaches, and fans alike.

Overall, Bican's rise to fame as a prolific goal scorer was a result of his natural talent, hard work, and dedication to the game. He was able to achieve things that few other players have, and his impact on the sport of football cannot be underestimated. His record-breaking achievements will always be remembered, and he will forever be regarded as one of the greatest goal scorers in football history.

Key achievements and records

Josef Bican is regarded as one of the greatest football players of all time, and his incredible goal-scoring record is a testament to his skill and talent on the field. In this chapter, we will explore some of his most significant achievements and records, which helped cement his legacy as a true legend of the game.

One of Bican's most notable achievements was his incredible goal-scoring record, which saw him score an astonishing 657 goals throughout his career. This included 545 goals at the club level and 112 goals at the national level, which are still among the highest goal-scoring records in football history.

Bican's most productive season came in 1948, when he scored an incredible 72 goals in just 41 matches. This feat remains unmatched to this day, and is a testament to Bican's incredible goal-scoring ability.

Bican was also known for his incredible speed and agility, which helped him to evade defenders and find the back of the net. His ability to dribble past multiple defenders and score from seemingly impossible angles made him a fan favorite and cemented his status as one of the greatest players of his era.

In addition to his impressive goal-scoring record, Bican also won numerous trophies and awards throughout his career. He won the Czechoslovak First League title on five occasions with Slavia Prague, and also helped the team to reach the final of the Mitropa Cup in 1938.

Bican was also named Czechoslovak Footballer of the Year twice, in 1952 and 1953. This award recognized his outstanding contributions to the national team and his incredible goal-scoring ability.

Overall, Josef Bican's achievements and records speak for themselves. He was a true master of the game and his incredible goal-scoring ability and agility on the field will always be remembered. His legacy continues to inspire future generations of football players, and his place among the greatest goal scorers in history is secure.

Legacy and impact on football

Josef Bican's legacy and impact on football cannot be overstated. His extraordinary goal-scoring prowess was not just an inspiration to aspiring football players, but it also changed the way people thought about the game.

Bican's legacy in football is multifaceted, and it extends beyond just his impressive statistics. He was a trailblazer for modern football, demonstrating how important the role of a goal scorer could be in a team's success. His achievements and records set the standard for future generations to aspire to and broke down many barriers and misconceptions about the sport.

One of Bican's most significant legacies is his impact on Czechoslovakia football. His performances for Rapid Vienna and Slavia Prague helped put Czech football on the map, and he is still regarded as one of the greatest Czech footballers of all time. His success paved the way for future generations of Czech players, and he continues to inspire young footballers to this day.

Bican's impact on football is also evident in his numerous records and achievements. He is still the all-time leading goal scorer in the history of Czechoslovakia's top-flight league, with 395 goals in just 217 matches. He also holds the record for the most goals in a single season in the Czechoslovak First League, with 57 goals in just 26 matches.

Bican's international record is also impressive, with 34 goals in just 42 appearances for Czechoslovakia. He was a key player in the Czechoslovak team that won the silver medal at the 1934 World Cup, scoring four goals in the tournament.

Beyond his impressive statistics, Bican's impact on football can be felt in the way he played the game. He was a versatile player, capable of playing in multiple positions, and he had an incredible sense of timing, which allowed him to be in the right place at the right time. His style of play was not just about scoring goals but about creating them as well, and he was known for his unselfish play and his ability to bring his teammates into the game.

Bican's legacy extends beyond the Czech Republic and into the wider footballing world. He is regarded as one of the greatest players of all time and is frequently mentioned in discussions of the greatest goal scorers in football history. His impact on the game has been felt across the globe, and his achievements continue to inspire generations of football players.

In conclusion, Josef Bican's legacy in football is unparalleled. He was a trailblazer for modern football, demonstrating the importance of a goal scorer to a team's success. His achievements and records set the standard for future generations to aspire to and his impact on the game can still be felt to this day. Bican's legacy is a testament to his incredible talent, hard work, and dedication to the sport of football.

Chapter 2: Eusebio - Portugal - 621 goals (473 club + 148 national) - retired 1979

Childhood and early football career

Eusebio, one of Portugal's greatest footballers of all time, was born on January 25, 1942, in Maputo, Mozambique. He grew up in the modest neighbourhood of Mafalala, where he developed a love for football at an early age. In Mafalala, children played football in the streets with homemade balls made of old rags or plastic bags. Eusebio was no exception, and he quickly showed his natural talent and ability on the football field.

Eusebio's family was poor, and he had to work hard to support himself and his family. He started working at a young age, shining shoes and selling peanuts to make a living. However, his passion for football never waned, and he continued to play in local tournaments and matches, catching the eye of several local coaches.

At the age of 15, Eusebio was recruited by Sporting de Lourenco Marques, a local football club. He quickly impressed his coaches and teammates with his speed, dribbling skills, and shooting ability. Despite his young age, he became a regular in the team, scoring numerous goals and helping his team win several trophies.

Eusebio's talent soon caught the attention of Benfica, one of Portugal's biggest football clubs. In 1960, Benfica offered him a contract, and Eusebio moved to Lisbon to begin his professional career. It was a big step for the young Mozambican, who had never been outside of Africa before.

Eusebio's first season at Benfica was a success, and he quickly became a fan favourite. His speed, skill, and powerful shot made him a formidable opponent, and he soon established himself as one of the best players in the Portuguese league. In the 1961-62 season, Eusebio helped Benfica win the Portuguese league title and the European Cup, scoring two goals in the final against Real Madrid.

Eusebio's success continued in the following years, and he won numerous individual awards, including the Ballon d'Or in 1965. He also led Portugal to a third-place finish in the 1966 World Cup, where he finished as the tournament's top scorer with nine goals.

Throughout his career, Eusebio remained humble and dedicated to his craft. He was known for his work ethic and his commitment to his team, and he always gave his best on the field. His talent and success inspired a generation of young footballers in Portugal and around the world.

Eusebio's childhood and early football career shaped him into the player and person he became. His hard work, determination, and natural talent propelled him to the heights of footballing success, and his impact on Portuguese football and culture is still felt today.

Success with Benfica and national team

Eusébio da Silva Ferreira, commonly known simply as Eusébio, was a Portuguese footballer who is widely considered to be one of the greatest players of all time. He is best known for his success with Benfica and the Portuguese national team, where he became a prolific scorer and led his teams to numerous victories. In this section, we will discuss Eusébio's success with Benfica and the Portuguese national team.

Success with Benfica

Eusébio joined Benfica in 1960, and quickly established himself as one of the most talented players in the team. He helped lead Benfica to numerous victories, including 11 Primeira Liga titles and the 1961 and 1962 European Cups. During his time at Benfica, Eusébio became known for his incredible speed and powerful shots, as well as his ability to score goals from seemingly impossible angles.

In the 1963/64 season, Eusébio had one of his most successful seasons with Benfica, scoring an incredible 43 goals in just 28 league games. This included two goals in the European Cup final against Inter Milan, which helped Benfica win the trophy for the second time in three years. Eusébio was also named the European Footballer of the Year in 1965, further cementing his status as one of the best players in the world.

Success with the Portuguese national team

Eusébio also had tremendous success with the Portuguese national team, helping to lead them to a third-place finish in the 1966 World Cup. During the tournament, he scored nine goals in six games, including four goals in a 5-3 victory over North Korea in the quarterfinals. His performance in the tournament earned him the Golden Boot as the top scorer and the Golden Ball as the best player.

Eusébio's success with the national team helped to raise the profile of Portuguese football and inspire a new generation of players. He continued to play for the national team until 1973, scoring a total of 41 goals in 64 appearances.

Legacy

Eusébio's success with Benfica and the Portuguese national team helped to establish him as one of the greatest footballers of all time. He was known for his incredible skill, speed, and power, as well as his ability to score goals from almost any position on the pitch. His impact on Portuguese football was immense, inspiring a generation of players and helping to raise the profile of the sport in Portugal.

After his retirement from football, Eusébio continued to be involved in the sport, working as an ambassador for

Benfica and the Portuguese national team. He passed away in 2014 at the age of 71, but his legacy in football lives on. He is remembered as one of the greatest goal scorers of all time, and his achievements continue to inspire footballers around the world.

Performance at the 1966 World Cup

Eusébio's performance at the 1966 World Cup in England is considered one of the most memorable performances by an individual player in the history of the tournament. Portugal was drawn into Group 3 alongside Hungary, Brazil, and Bulgaria. They kicked off their campaign with a 3-1 loss to Hungary in their opening match, with Eusébio scoring Portugal's only goal from the penalty spot.

In their next game against Bulgaria, Eusébio netted twice to help Portugal to a 3-0 victory. However, it was their third and final group game against Brazil that would become the most famous match of Eusébio's career.

Brazil was one of the favorites to win the tournament and featured some of the best players in the world at the time, including Pelé. Portugal had never beaten Brazil before, and few gave them much of a chance heading into the game.

Despite being labeled as underdogs, Portugal started the game brightly and took a shock lead through José Augusto. Brazil equalized before half-time, but Portugal restored their lead through Eusébio early in the second half. Brazil leveled once again before Eusébio scored his second goal of the game from the penalty spot.

With Portugal leading 3-2, Brazil threw everything forward in search of an equalizer, but Eusébio put the game to bed with a stunning long-range strike that flew into the top corner of the net. The goal became known as the "Goal of the Century" and is still considered one of the greatest goals in World Cup history.

Eusébio's heroics in that game helped Portugal to reach the semi-finals of the World Cup for the first time in their history, where they were beaten by eventual champions England. Despite the disappointment of missing out on a place in the final, Eusébio had announced himself on the world stage and was awarded the Golden Boot for being the tournament's top scorer with nine goals.

Eusébio's performances at the 1966 World Cup not only helped Portugal to achieve their best-ever finish at the tournament, but they also earned him worldwide recognition as one of the greatest players of his generation. His stunning goal against Brazil is still talked about to this day and is considered one of the greatest moments in World Cup history.

Legacy and impact on Portuguese football

Eusebio, who is widely regarded as one of the greatest football players of all time, left a lasting legacy on the game in Portugal. Not only did he inspire future generations of Portuguese footballers, but he also helped put Portuguese football on the map on the international stage. In this section, we will explore Eusebio's legacy and his impact on Portuguese football.

Eusebio's impact on Portuguese football began during his playing career, particularly in the 1960s, when he played for Benfica and the Portuguese national team. During this time, Portuguese football was still relatively unknown on the global stage. However, Eusebio's success with Benfica, particularly in winning the European Cup in 1961 and 1962, helped raise the profile of Portuguese football. Furthermore, his performances for the national team helped put Portugal on the map in international football.

Eusebio's success on the pitch was accompanied by a larger-than-life personality off the pitch. He was a charismatic figure who was beloved by fans in Portugal and around the world. His natural talent and humble personality made him a role model for young footballers in Portugal, who aspired to follow in his footsteps.

After retiring from football in 1979, Eusebio continued to be an important figure in Portuguese football. He worked as an ambassador for Benfica and the Portuguese Football Federation, promoting the sport in Portugal and around the world. He also played an important role in the development of young footballers in Portugal, serving as a mentor and inspiration to many.

Eusebio's legacy in Portuguese football has been cemented in the years since his death in 2014. He remains a beloved figure in Portuguese football, and his impact on the game is still felt today. Many of the current generation of Portuguese footballers, such as Cristiano Ronaldo, have cited Eusebio as an inspiration and role model.

One of the ways in which Eusebio's legacy is celebrated in Portugal is through the annual Eusebio Cup, a pre-season friendly match between Benfica and a selected team from around the world. The match is held in honor of Eusebio and is a celebration of his life and achievements.

In addition to the Eusebio Cup, there are numerous other ways in which Eusebio's legacy is celebrated in Portugal. Statues and memorials have been erected in his honor, and he has been featured on numerous postage stamps and coins. Furthermore, the Eusebio Foundation, established after his death, works to promote football and support underprivileged children in Portugal.

In conclusion, Eusebio's impact on Portuguese football is immeasurable. He helped raise the profile of Portuguese football on the global stage, inspired future generations of footballers, and left a lasting legacy that is still celebrated today. His natural talent, humble personality, and larger-than-life persona make him one of the most beloved figures in the history of Portuguese football.

Chapter 3: Leônidas - Brazil - 358 goals (344 club + 14 national) - retired 1942

Early life and rise to fame

Leônidas da Silva, also known as "Diamante Negro" (Black Diamond), is considered one of the greatest Brazilian footballers of all time. He was born on September 6, 1913, in Rio de Janeiro, Brazil. Leônidas grew up in poverty and started playing football at a young age on the streets of his hometown.

Early Life and Football Career Beginnings

Leônidas' family could not afford to send him to school, so he worked odd jobs to make ends meet. His love for football was evident from a young age, and he would often spend hours playing with his friends. He developed his skills on the streets and quickly gained a reputation as a talented young player.

At the age of 15, Leônidas was spotted by a local club, Bonsucesso, and was invited to join their youth team. He impressed the coaches with his technical ability and speed, and soon he was promoted to the first team. Leônidas' performances for Bonsucesso caught the eye of other clubs, and he was soon signed by Vasco da Gama, one of the biggest clubs in Brazil.

Rise to Fame

Leônidas made his debut for Vasco da Gama in 1930, and it did not take him long to establish himself as one of the most exciting players in the league. He was a dynamic forward with excellent dribbling skills and an eye for goal. Leônidas was also known for his acrobatic ability and was one of the first players to introduce the bicycle kick to Brazilian football.

Leônidas' performances for Vasco da Gama earned him a call-up to the Brazilian national team. He made his debut for Brazil in 1932 and went on to represent his country in two World Cups (1934 and 1938). Leônidas was the top scorer of the 1938 World Cup, scoring seven goals in five matches.

Leônidas continued to play for Vasco da Gama until 1935 when he moved to Flamengo, one of the biggest clubs in Brazil. He spent two seasons at Flamengo before moving to São Paulo FC in 1937. At São Paulo, Leônidas won the São Paulo State Championship in 1938 and 1939.

Key Achievements and Records

Leônidas' achievements on the field are numerous. He won several domestic titles with Vasco da Gama, Flamengo, and São Paulo FC. He was also the top scorer of the São Paulo State Championship three times (1938, 1939, and 1942).

Leônidas' most significant achievement, however, came at the 1938 World Cup in France. He scored seven goals in five matches, including four in the quarterfinals against Poland. Leônidas was the driving force behind Brazil's campaign and helped them finish in third place.

Legacy and Impact on Football

Leônidas' impact on Brazilian football cannot be overstated. He was one of the first Brazilian players to gain international recognition and paved the way for the likes of Pelé, Garrincha, and Zico. Leônidas was also a trailblazer for black players in Brazil and helped break down racial barriers in the sport.

Leônidas' acrobatic ability and goal-scoring prowess inspired a generation of Brazilian players, and his name is still revered in the country today. In 1998, FIFA named him one of the 100 greatest players of all time, and he was posthumously inducted into the Brazilian Football Hall of Fame in 1977.

Leônidas' legacy continues to inspire young players in Brazil and around the world, and his contributions to the sport will never be forgotten.

Success with Flamengo and the Brazilian national team

Leônidas da Silva is widely considered one of the greatest Brazilian footballers of all time. His performances for both Flamengo and the Brazilian national team cemented his place in football history. In this section, we will explore Leônidas' success with Flamengo and the Brazilian national team, including his key achievements and records.

Success with Flamengo

Leônidas began his professional career with São Paulo-based club, Peñarol. However, it was his move to Rio de Janeiro giants, Flamengo, that would really put him on the map. He joined the club in 1936 and quickly became a fan favorite with his skillful dribbling, powerful shooting, and acrobatic ability.

Leônidas helped Flamengo win the Rio de Janeiro State Championship in 1939 and 1942, scoring 105 goals in 155 appearances for the club. One of his most famous goals for Flamengo came in a match against rivals Fluminense in 1942. With Flamengo trailing 3-0, Leônidas scored four goals in the final 20 minutes to secure a remarkable 4-3 victory.

Success with the Brazilian national team

Leônidas made his debut for the Brazilian national team in 1932 and went on to make 19 appearances, scoring

14 goals. He played a key role in Brazil's success at the 1938 World Cup in France, where he scored seven goals in five matches and helped Brazil finish in third place.

One of Leônidas' most famous goals came in Brazil's quarter-final match against Poland at the 1938 World Cup. With Brazil trailing 1-0, Leônidas equalized with a stunning bicycle kick. Brazil went on to win the match 6-5, with Leônidas scoring two more goals.

Leônidas' performance at the 1938 World Cup earned him the nickname "The Rubber Man" due to his ability to contort his body in mid-air to score acrobatic goals. He was also the tournament's top scorer and won the Bronze Ball award for being the third-best player of the tournament.

Key achievements and records

Leônidas' impact on Brazilian football cannot be overstated. He was a pioneer of Brazilian football and helped to establish the style of play that would later be known as "samba football". He was also a prolific goalscorer and holds a number of records for both Flamengo and the Brazilian national team.

Some of Leônidas' key achievements and records include:

- Top scorer of the 1938 World Cup (7 goals)
- Bronze Ball award winner at the 1938 World Cup

- Two-time winner of the Rio de Janeiro State Championship with Flamengo (1939, 1942)

- Scored 105 goals in 155 appearances for Flamengo

- Scored 14 goals in 19 appearances for the Brazilian national team

Legacy and impact on Brazilian football

Leônidas' impact on Brazilian football cannot be overstated. He was a pioneer of the attacking style of play that would later become synonymous with Brazilian football. His skill, technique, and acrobatic ability were unparalleled at the time and inspired a generation of Brazilian footballers.

Leônidas' success at the 1938 World Cup helped to establish Brazil as a major footballing nation and set the standard for future Brazilian teams. His acrobatic goals and flamboyant style of play captured the imagination of football fans around the world and helped to popularize Brazilian football.

Today, Leônidas is remembered as one of the greatest Brazilian footballers of all time. His impact on Brazilian football is still felt to this day, and his legacy lives on through the generations of Brazilian footballers who have followed in his footsteps.

Performance at the 1938 World Cup

Leônidas da Silva's performance at the 1938 World Cup is considered one of the greatest individual performances in the history of the tournament. Brazil entered the tournament as one of the favorites, but they faced a tough draw in the first round, being placed in a group with Czechoslovakia and Switzerland.

In the first match against Czechoslovakia, Leônidas was left out of the starting lineup due to an injury. However, with Brazil trailing 1-0 in the second half, he was brought on as a substitute and scored the equalizer with a powerful header. The match ended in a 1-1 draw, and Brazil needed to beat Switzerland in their final group match to advance to the quarterfinals.

Leônidas started the match against Switzerland and put in a sensational performance. He scored Brazil's first goal with a spectacular bicycle kick, which is considered one of the greatest goals in World Cup history. He then added a second goal, and Brazil went on to win the match 2-1 and advance to the quarterfinals.

In the quarterfinals, Brazil faced a tough match against Czechoslovakia, who had eliminated them in the previous World Cup. Leônidas was once again left out of the starting lineup due to injury, but he was brought on in the second half with Brazil trailing 1-0. He scored the equalizer with a powerful shot, and Brazil went on to win the match 2-1 and advance to the semifinals.

In the semifinals, Brazil faced Italy, who were the reigning World Cup champions. Leônidas put in another outstanding performance and scored Brazil's only goal in the match, but it wasn't enough, as Italy won 2-1 and advanced to the final.

Despite Brazil's defeat in the semifinals, Leônidas was awarded the Golden Boot for being the top scorer of the tournament, with seven goals in four matches. He was also named the best player of the tournament by the French sports newspaper, L'Équipe.

Leônidas' performance at the 1938 World Cup established him as one of the greatest players of his generation and cemented his legacy as a Brazilian football legend. His spectacular bicycle kick goal against Switzerland is still considered one of the greatest goals in World Cup history, and his seven-goal tally in the tournament stood as a record for over 20 years. His impact on Brazilian football can still be felt today, as he inspired a generation of Brazilian players who went on to win five World Cup titles.

Legacy and impact on Brazilian football

Leônidas da Silva, also known as "The Black Diamond", left a lasting legacy on Brazilian football that is still felt today. His contributions to the sport, both on and off the pitch, have helped shape Brazilian football into what it is today. In this section, we will explore Leônidas' legacy and impact on Brazilian football.

Revolutionizing Brazilian Football

Leônidas was one of the first players to bring a new style of play to Brazilian football. His quick and agile movements, combined with his powerful shots and acrobatic skills, helped revolutionize the game. He introduced a new level of technical skill that was previously unseen in Brazil, inspiring younger players to follow in his footsteps.

His influence was felt both on and off the pitch. Leônidas was an ambassador for the sport, and he helped bring attention to Brazilian football on the international stage. He was a role model for many young Brazilians, and his achievements gave hope to those who dreamed of playing professionally.

A National Hero

Leônidas' performances at the 1938 World Cup cemented his status as a national hero. His four goals in the tournament helped Brazil reach the semifinals, and his performances were praised by fans and media alike. He was awarded the Golden Boot as the tournament's top scorer, and his bicycle kick against Poland was named the "most beautiful goal in the history of the World Cup."

Leônidas' success at the World Cup helped raise the profile of Brazilian football around the world. He became a household name, and his achievements inspired a generation of young players in Brazil.

Influence on Brazilian Football Culture

Leônidas' impact on Brazilian football culture was significant. He helped popularize the sport, and his performances inspired a new generation of fans. His skills and techniques were studied by young players across Brazil, and his legacy helped shape the country's football culture.

His contributions to the sport were recognized by the Brazilian government, which awarded him the Order of Merit in 1995. He was also posthumously inducted into the Brazilian Football Museum Hall of Fame, and his name is forever etched in the history of Brazilian football.

Conclusion

Leônidas da Silva was a true legend of Brazilian football. His impact on the sport is still felt today, and his contributions helped shape Brazilian football into what it is today. He was a trailblazer, introducing a new level of technical skill to the game and inspiring a generation of young players. He will forever be remembered as one of the greatest players in the history of Brazilian football.

Chapter 4: Gyula Zsengellér - Hungary - 354 goals (338 club + 16 national) - retired 1942

Early life and football career beginnings

Gyula Zsengellér was a Hungarian footballer who is widely regarded as one of the greatest goal scorers of all time. Born on March 27, 1915, in Budapest, Hungary, he grew up in a family of football enthusiasts, with his father and uncle both being former players.

Zsengellér started his football career at the age of 10, playing for a local team called Kispest AC. He quickly made a name for himself with his impressive skills on the field and soon caught the attention of larger clubs in Hungary.

At the age of 16, Zsengellér was signed by the Budapest-based club, MTK Budapest FC, which was one of the most successful teams in Hungary at the time. He made his first-team debut for the club in 1932 and quickly established himself as a regular in the team.

Rise to Fame as a Prolific Goal Scorer

Zsengellér's rise to fame as a prolific goal scorer began in the 1933-34 season when he scored an impressive 28 goals in 26 league matches for MTK Budapest FC. This was the first of many goal-scoring feats for Zsengellér, and he soon became known as one of the deadliest finishers in Europe.

Over the next few years, Zsengellér continued to score at an incredible rate, both for MTK Budapest FC and the Hungarian national team. He was a key player for Hungary during their golden era in the 1930s, when they won the Central European International Cup three times and finished runners-up at the 1938 FIFA World Cup.

Key Achievements and Records

Zsengellér's record as a goal scorer is truly remarkable. He scored a total of 354 goals in his career, including 338 for his club and 16 for the national team. This puts him in fourth place on the all-time list of Hungarian goal scorers.

One of Zsengellér's most impressive achievements was his scoring record in the Hungarian League. He scored a total of 327 goals in just 296 league matches, making him the highest-scoring player in the history of the league.

Zsengellér was also a key player for Hungary at the 1938 FIFA World Cup. He scored four goals in the tournament, including a hat-trick against Sweden in the quarter-finals. Although Hungary eventually finished as runners-up, Zsengellér's performances helped to establish him as one of the best players in the world at the time.

Legacy and Impact on Football

Zsengellér's impact on Hungarian football cannot be overstated. He was a key player for Hungary during their most successful era in the 1930s and helped to establish the country as a major force in international football.

Zsengellér's goal-scoring prowess also inspired a generation of Hungarian players who would go on to achieve great success in the sport. His record in the Hungarian League still stands to this day and is a testament to his incredible ability as a goal scorer.

Outside of Hungary, Zsengellér's impact was also felt. His performances at the 1938 FIFA World Cup helped to establish him as one of the best players in the world at the time, and his goal-scoring feats continue to inspire players and fans alike to this day.

In conclusion, Gyula Zsengellér was one of the greatest goal scorers of all time, and his impact on Hungarian football cannot be overstated. His record as a goal scorer is truly remarkable, and his legacy as a player continues to inspire future generations of footballers.

Rise to fame as a goal scorer in Hungary and Austria

Gyula Zsengellér was born on 27 November 1915 in Budapest, Hungary. He began playing football at a young age, and by the time he was a teenager, he had joined the youth teams of Budapest-based club Ferencvárosi TC, one of Hungary's most successful clubs.

Rise to Fame in Hungary

Zsengellér made his senior debut for Ferencvárosi in 1933, at the age of 18. In his early years, he struggled to establish himself in the first team, but he continued to work hard and improve his game. By the mid-1930s, he had become a regular in the side and was beginning to make a name for himself as a goal scorer.

During the 1937-38 season, Zsengellér established himself as one of the top goal scorers in Hungary. He scored 36 goals in 30 league matches, helping Ferencvárosi win the Hungarian league title. He also scored five goals in the Hungarian Cup, including two in the final, as Ferencvárosi won the double.

The following season, Zsengellér continued his impressive form, scoring 43 goals in 32 league matches. He was the league's top scorer for the second consecutive season, and Ferencvárosi won the league title for the second year in a row. Zsengellér's performances earned him a call-up to the Hungarian national team, and he made his debut in 1938.

Move to Austria

In 1939, Zsengellér was sold to Austrian club First Vienna FC for a record fee of 250,000 pengő. At the time, this was the highest transfer fee ever paid for a Hungarian player.

Zsengellér quickly established himself as a key player for First Vienna. In his first season, he scored 23 goals in 23 league matches, helping the club win the Austrian championship. He was also the league's top scorer, despite playing in only half of the matches due to his late arrival in the season.

Over the next few seasons, Zsengellér continued to excel in Austria, scoring goals at an incredible rate. In the 1940-41 season, he scored 37 goals in 24 league matches, once again finishing as the league's top scorer. He helped First Vienna win the Austrian Cup in 1941, scoring the winning goal in the final.

During his time in Austria, Zsengellér became known for his exceptional goal-scoring ability, his speed, and his agility. He was also admired for his technical skills and his ability to create chances for his teammates.

International Success

Zsengellér's performances in Austria earned him a recall to the Hungarian national team in 1940. He quickly established himself as one of Hungary's most important players, helping the team win the Balkan Cup in 1940 and 1941.

In 1942, Zsengellér played a key role in Hungary's successful campaign in the Central European International Cup, a competition involving Hungary, Germany, Italy, and Croatia. Zsengellér scored four goals in five matches, helping Hungary win the tournament.

Retirement

Zsengellér retired from football in 1942, at the age of 27. He had scored a total of 354 goals in his career, including 338 at club level and 16 for the Hungarian national team. He remained in Austria after his retirement and became a successful coach.

Zsengellér is remembered as one of the greatest Hungarian footballers of all time. His goal-scoring ability, pace, and skill made him a legend in Hungary and Austria, and he was highly respected by both fans and players alike. He was a key player in the legendary Hungarian team of the 1930s, which is widely regarded as one of the greatest national teams of all time. Zsengellér was also highly successful in club football, winning multiple league titles with Ferencvárosi TC in Hungary and Austria Vienna. His performances in Europe also caught the attention of other top European clubs, including Juventus and FC Barcelona, who both attempted to sign him at various points in his career. In this section, we will delve into Zsengellér's rise to fame as a goal scorer in Hungary and Austria, tracing his early years and his development as a player, before examining his achievements and legacy in greater detail.

Success with the Hungarian national team

Gyula Zsengellér's success with the Hungarian national team was perhaps the most significant achievement of his career. He made his debut for Hungary in 1929 and went on to become a key player for the national team, earning a total of 43 caps and scoring 16 goals.

One of his earliest successes with the national team came in the 1934 World Cup, held in Italy. Although Hungary was knocked out in the first round, Zsengellér managed to score two goals in their opening match against Egypt, helping his team to a 4-2 victory. Despite Hungary's early exit from the tournament, Zsengellér's performances had caught the attention of football fans across Europe.

Zsengellér's most notable success with the national team came in the 1938 World Cup, held in France. He was the top scorer of the tournament, scoring a total of six goals in just four games. Hungary made it all the way to the final, where they faced Italy in what would become known as the "Battle of Paris". The match was marred by violent incidents and allegations of biased refereeing, but Zsengellér managed to score Hungary's only goal in the 8-1 defeat.

Despite the loss in the final, Zsengellér's performances in the tournament earned him widespread recognition as one of the best footballers in the world. He was named in the World Cup All-Star Team, becoming the first Hungarian player to receive this honor. His six goals in the tournament also saw him awarded the Golden Boot, an accolade given to the tournament's top scorer.

Zsengellér's success with the national team continued after the World Cup, as Hungary embarked on a record-breaking run of 31 consecutive unbeaten matches between 1938 and 1942. Zsengellér played a key role in this run, scoring 14 goals in 20 matches.

Unfortunately, Zsengellér's international career was cut short by the outbreak of World War II. Hungary did not participate in the 1946 World Cup, and Zsengellér retired from international football soon after.

Despite his relatively short international career, Zsengellér's impact on Hungarian football was profound. He was instrumental in Hungary's successes in the 1930s, and his performances helped to establish Hungary as one of the dominant footballing nations of the era. His goal-scoring ability and skill on the ball made him a hero to Hungarian football fans, and his legacy continues to inspire new generations of players in Hungary and beyond.

Legacy and impact on Hungarian football

Gyula Zsengellér's legacy in Hungarian football is immense. He is remembered as one of the greatest players to have ever played for the Hungarian national team and one of the country's all-time leading goal scorers. Zsengellér's contribution to Hungary's footballing success in the 1930s was significant, and his influence is still felt in the country's footballing culture today.

One of Zsengellér's most significant impacts on Hungarian football was his role in the team's successful tour of Italy in 1933. The Hungarian national team had never beaten Italy before, but Zsengellér's three goals in the match helped secure a 3-2 victory. This historic win was a turning point for Hungarian football, and it helped establish the national team as a serious contender in international football.

Zsengellér was also a member of the famous Hungarian "Golden Team" of the 1930s, which included other legendary players such as Ferenc Puskás and Zoltán Czibor. The team was known for its innovative tactics and fluid style of play, which revolutionized football at the time. Zsengellér's contribution to the team's success cannot be understated, and his skill and goal-scoring prowess helped elevate the Hungarian national team to new heights.

Off the pitch, Zsengellér was also influential in Hungarian football. After retiring from playing, he became a successful coach and managed several Hungarian clubs, including Ferencváros, where he helped the team win the Hungarian League in 1949. Zsengellér's coaching style was characterized by his innovative ideas and his focus on attacking football, which helped inspire a new generation of Hungarian footballers.

Zsengellér's impact on Hungarian football was recognized by the country's footballing authorities, and he was inducted into the Hungarian Football Hall of Fame in 2005. His legacy continues to inspire Hungarian footballers today, and he is remembered as a symbol of Hungary's footballing success in the 1930s.

In conclusion, Gyula Zsengellér's contribution to Hungarian football cannot be understated. His goal-scoring ability and skill on the pitch made him one of the greatest players of his generation, and his influence off the pitch helped inspire a new generation of Hungarian footballers. Zsengellér's legacy continues to inspire and motivate Hungarian footballers today, and he will always be remembered as one of the greatest players to have ever played for the Hungarian national team.

Chapter 5: Sándor Kocsis - Hungary - 331 goals (257 club + 74 national) - retired 1961

Childhood and early football career

Sándor Kocsis was born on September 21, 1929, in Budapest, Hungary. He was the youngest of three children in his family. Kocsis grew up playing football on the streets of Budapest with his older brother, Ferenc. His talent quickly became apparent, and he joined the youth team of Ferencvárosi TC at the age of 12.

Kocsis' skills as a striker were evident from a young age, and he quickly rose through the ranks of the Ferencvárosi TC youth system. By the time he was 16 years old, he had made his debut for the senior team. Despite his age, he immediately made an impact, scoring two goals in his first game.

Kocsis continued to impress for Ferencvárosi TC, and in the 1949-50 season, he was the top scorer in the Hungarian league, with 36 goals in 29 games. This remarkable feat helped his team win the league title that season.

Kocsis' performances for Ferencvárosi TC did not go unnoticed, and in 1950 he was selected to represent Hungary at the World Cup in Brazil. Despite being just 21 years old, Kocsis played a key role in Hungary's run to the final, scoring four goals in the tournament. Although Hungary lost to Uruguay in the final, Kocsis had established himself as one of the most promising young players in world football.

Following the World Cup, Kocsis continued to excel for Ferencvárosi TC. In the 1951-52 season, he scored an incredible 38 goals in just 28 games, helping his team win another league title. He was also named Hungarian Footballer of the Year in 1952, an honor he would win two more times in his career.

Kocsis' success with Ferencvárosi TC earned him a move to Barcelona in 1958, where he would play alongside fellow Hungarian legend, László Kubala. Kocsis' time at Barcelona was brief, but he still managed to score an impressive 23 goals in just 26 games.

Throughout his career, Kocsis was known for his incredible aerial ability and clinical finishing. He had a knack for finding space in the box and was lethal with both his head and his feet. He was also known for his strength and physicality, making him a nightmare for defenders to mark.

Kocsis retired from football in 1961, at the age of 32. In total, he scored 331 goals in his career, including 74 for the Hungarian national team. He remains one of the greatest Hungarian footballers of all time, and his legacy continues to inspire young players in Hungary and beyond.

Success with Honved and the Hungarian national team

Sándor Kocsis is known as one of the greatest Hungarian footballers of all time, having achieved tremendous success with Honved and the Hungarian national team. After joining Honved in 1945, Kocsis quickly established himself as a prolific goal scorer, leading the team to numerous domestic titles. His ability to score goals with both feet and his aerial prowess made him a feared opponent for any defense.

Kocsis made his debut for the Hungarian national team in 1948, and he quickly established himself as one of the team's key players. He played a crucial role in Hungary's famous 6-3 victory over England at Wembley Stadium in 1953, scoring three goals in the match. Kocsis was part of the Hungarian team that won a gold medal at the 1952 Olympics, and he helped lead Hungary to the final of the 1954 World Cup.

At the 1954 World Cup, Kocsis had a phenomenal tournament, scoring a total of 11 goals, including two hat-tricks. His performance at the tournament earned him the Golden Boot as the top scorer, and he was named to the tournament's All-Star Team. Despite Hungary's disappointment in losing to West Germany in the final,

Kocsis's performance at the tournament cemented his status as one of the greatest players in Hungarian football history.

Kocsis continued to play for the Hungarian national team until 1956, when he was forced to flee the country following the Hungarian Revolution. He retired from international football with 75 caps and 75 goals, a remarkable goal-scoring record that still stands today.

In addition to his success with Honved and the Hungarian national team, Kocsis also had a successful career with FC Barcelona in Spain. He joined the club in 1958 and helped lead them to two La Liga titles and a Fairs Cup victory. Kocsis retired from football in 1961 at the age of 37, having scored a total of 331 goals in his career.

Kocsis's legacy in Hungarian football is immense. His goal-scoring record for the national team still stands, and he is widely regarded as one of the greatest players in the country's history. His performance at the 1954 World Cup is still remembered as one of the greatest individual performances in the history of the tournament, and his ability to score goals from anywhere on the field was a testament to his skill and determination. Kocsis's impact on Hungarian football will never be forgotten, and he will always be remembered as a true legend of the game.

Performance at the 1954 World Cup

The 1954 World Cup was a defining moment in Sándor Kocsis' career. Hungary entered the tournament as one of the favorites, having recently defeated England 6-3 in a historic match at Wembley Stadium. Kocsis was a key player in Hungary's "Golden Team," which had gone unbeaten in 31 matches prior to the World Cup.

In Hungary's opening match against South Korea, Kocsis scored twice in a 9-0 victory. He then added two more goals in a 8-3 win over West Germany. In the quarterfinals, Kocsis scored the opening goal in a 4-2 win over Brazil, helping Hungary advance to the semifinals.

In the semifinals, Hungary faced Uruguay in what would become known as the "Battle of Berne." The match was marred by violence, with both teams engaging in physical altercations on the field. Despite the chaos, Kocsis managed to score a goal in the 2-2 draw. Hungary advanced to the final on goal difference, where they would face West Germany in a rematch.

In the final, Kocsis scored again, giving Hungary an early 1-0 lead. However, West Germany would mount a comeback, scoring twice in the second half to win the match 3-2. Despite the loss, Kocsis finished the tournament as its top scorer with 11 goals in just 5 matches.

Kocsis' performance at the 1954 World Cup cemented his place as one of the greatest players of his generation. He was named to the tournament's All-Star Team and won the Golden Boot as its top scorer. His 11 goals in a single World Cup remained a record until 2006, when it was broken by Miroslav Klose.

The 1954 World Cup also had a significant impact on Hungarian football. Despite their loss in the final, Hungary's "Golden Team" was widely regarded as one of the greatest football teams in history. Their innovative tactics, known as the "Magical Magyars," helped revolutionize the sport and influenced generations of players and coaches.

Kocsis' performance in the tournament was a key part of Hungary's success, and his legacy as a goal-scoring machine was firmly established. He would go on to play in the 1958 World Cup before retiring from international football with 75 goals in just 68 matches, a scoring rate that remains unmatched to this day.

Legacy and impact on Hungarian football

Sándor Kocsis left an indelible mark on Hungarian football during his career and beyond. His achievements on the pitch and his contributions to the national team's golden era have earned him a lasting legacy as one of Hungary's greatest footballers of all time.

Kocsis' prolific goal-scoring record and his role in Hungary's iconic 1953 and 1954 victories over England and Uruguay, respectively, made him an iconic figure in Hungarian football. However, his legacy extends beyond his performances on the pitch.

Kocsis was known for his modest and unassuming personality, which earned him the nickname "Golden Head" and endeared him to fans and teammates alike. He was a true gentleman of the sport, admired for his integrity and sportsmanship both on and off the field.

Following his playing career, Kocsis became a coach and continued to contribute to Hungarian football. He led several Hungarian clubs, including Ferencváros and MTK Budapest, and helped develop the next generation of Hungarian footballers.

Beyond his impact on Hungarian football, Kocsis' legacy also extends to the sport as a whole. He was a pioneer in the use of specialized training methods and sports psychology, emphasizing the importance of mental and physical preparation for optimal performance.

Kocsis' lasting impact on Hungarian football is evident in the numerous honors and tributes he has received. In 2001, he was named Hungary's Footballer of the Century, and his name has been immortalized in the country's national football stadium, which was renamed the Puskás Ferenc Stadium in honor of his former teammate.

Overall, Sándor Kocsis' legacy as a player, coach, and innovator has left an enduring imprint on Hungarian football and continues to inspire future generations of players and coaches. His contributions to the sport both on and off the field have earned him a well-deserved place in the annals of football history.

Chapter 6: Jimmy Greaves - England - 297 goals (268 club + 29 national) - retired 1971

Early life and rise to fame at Chelsea

Jimmy Greaves was born on February 20, 1940, in Manor Park, East London, England. He grew up in a working-class family and began playing football at a young age. He quickly showed his talent for the sport and was soon scouted by several local clubs.

At the age of just 15, Greaves signed for Chelsea, one of the biggest clubs in England. He made his debut for the first team just a year later, in 1957, at the age of 17. Despite his youth, Greaves quickly made an impact on the team and became their top scorer in his first season. He went on to become the league's top scorer in the following two seasons, scoring an impressive 32 goals in the 1958-59 season and 41 goals in the 1959-60 season.

Greaves' goalscoring prowess quickly made him a fan favorite at Stamford Bridge, and he became known for his ability to score from almost any position on the pitch. His lightning-fast pace, quick feet, and clinical finishing made him one of the most exciting young players in the country.

Greaves helped Chelsea win the league championship in the 1954-55 season, and he continued to score prolifically for the club until he was sold to Italian giants AC Milan in

1961. In his time at Chelsea, Greaves scored an incredible 132 league goals in just 169 appearances, making him one of the club's all-time greats.

Despite his success at Chelsea, Greaves' career was far from over. He went on to play for a number of other clubs, including Tottenham Hotspur, West Ham United, and Barnet, scoring goals wherever he went. However, it was at Tottenham that Greaves enjoyed some of his greatest success, winning two FA Cups and the European Cup Winners' Cup.

Overall, Greaves' early life and rise to fame at Chelsea set the stage for what would become a legendary career. His incredible talent and natural ability to score goals made him one of the most exciting players to watch in English football, and his impact on the game would be felt for many years to come.

Success with Tottenham and the English national team

Jimmy Greaves' success with Tottenham Hotspur and the English national team cemented his status as one of the greatest footballers of his generation.

In 1961, Greaves transferred to Tottenham Hotspur for a then-record fee of £99,999. He immediately became a fan favorite, scoring 37 goals in his first season with the club. In total, he scored 266 goals in 379 appearances for Tottenham, helping the team win two FA Cups, the European Cup Winners' Cup, and the First Division title in 1961.

Greaves also had a successful international career, scoring 44 goals in 57 appearances for the England national team. He made his debut in 1959, and quickly established himself as a key player for the team. His partnership with Bobby Charlton was particularly fruitful, and the two scored a total of 49 goals in the 38 matches they played together.

One of Greaves' most memorable performances for England came in a match against Italy in 1961. He scored all four goals in England's 4-1 victory, becoming the first player to score four goals in a match for the national team since 1938. He also played a crucial role in England's successful

1966 World Cup campaign, scoring five goals in the qualifying rounds to help the team reach the finals.

Despite his impressive goal-scoring record, Greaves' international career was cut short in 1966 due to an injury sustained during a match against France. He was replaced by Geoff Hurst, who went on to score a hat-trick in England's 4-2 victory over West Germany in the World Cup final. Greaves received a winner's medal for his contribution to the team's success, but many believe that he would have played a more significant role had he not been injured.

Greaves' success with Tottenham and England earned him numerous accolades, including the Football Writers' Association Footballer of the Year award in 1961 and 1967, and the PFA Players' Player of the Year award in 1961. He was also included in the England team of the century in 2003, and inducted into the English Football Hall of Fame in 2002.

Greaves' style of play, which combined lightning-fast pace, exceptional skill, and deadly accuracy in front of goal, inspired a generation of young footballers in England and around the world. His legacy as one of the greatest goal-scorers in English football history is undisputed, and his impact on the sport is still felt to this day.

Controversy and struggles later in his career

Jimmy Greaves was one of the most prolific goal scorers in English football history, but his career was not without its controversies and struggles. In the latter stages of his career, Greaves faced a number of challenges both on and off the pitch that impacted his performances.

One of the major controversies that surrounded Greaves was his exclusion from the England squad for the 1966 World Cup. Despite scoring an impressive 44 goals in 57 appearances for his country, Greaves was not selected for the tournament. Many speculated that this was due to a personal disagreement with the England manager, Alf Ramsey. Greaves himself later revealed that he was struggling with depression at the time, which may have also played a role in his exclusion from the squad.

After the disappointment of the World Cup, Greaves continued to play for Tottenham but found himself struggling to maintain his form. Injuries and illnesses also took their toll, and he was forced to miss a number of games. In the 1968-69 season, Greaves made just 11 league appearances and scored only three goals. Despite this, he was still able to contribute to Tottenham's success in the FA Cup that season, scoring in the final against Leicester City.

In 1970, Greaves moved to West Ham United, but his struggles continued. He found it difficult to break into the first team and was also dealing with personal problems, including issues with alcohol. In March 1971, Greaves was involved in a serious car accident that left him with a broken leg and ankle. He was forced to retire from professional football at the age of just 31.

After retiring, Greaves struggled with alcoholism and depression. He was open about his struggles and worked hard to overcome them. He also became a successful television pundit and commentator, known for his wit and humor. In 2009, he was honored with an MBE for his services to football.

Despite the challenges he faced later in his career, Greaves is still remembered as one of the greatest goal scorers in English football history. His total of 357 goals in the top flight of English football is the fourth-highest of all time, and his 44 goals for England still rank him as the fourth-highest scorer for the national team. His speed, agility, and clinical finishing made him a joy to watch on the pitch, and he inspired a generation of young players with his performances.

Legacy and impact on English football

Introduction: Jimmy Greaves is considered one of the greatest goal-scorers in English football history. His record of 357 league goals stood for over 50 years until it was broken in 2019. In this section, we will discuss Greaves' legacy and his impact on English football.

Greaves' Goal-Scoring Record: Greaves' goal-scoring record speaks for itself. He scored 357 league goals in just 516 games, a remarkable average of 0.69 goals per game. He was also the youngest player to score 100 league goals, accomplishing the feat at just 20 years old. His record of 44 goals in a single season, set in the 1960-61 season, stood for 39 years until it was broken by Clive Allen in 1980.

Success with Tottenham: Greaves' success with Tottenham is well documented. He scored 266 goals in 379 appearances for the club, helping them win two FA Cups and the European Cup Winners' Cup. In the 1960-61 season, Greaves scored 37 league goals, helping Tottenham win the league title. He also formed a formidable partnership with fellow striker Bobby Smith, which was instrumental in Tottenham's success.

Greaves and the England National Team: Greaves played for the England national team between 1959 and 1967, scoring 44 goals in 57 appearances. He is still the fourth-highest goal-scorer in the history of the England national team. Greaves played a key role in England's 1966 World Cup win, although he missed the latter stages of the tournament due to injury. It is widely believed that had Greaves been fit for the final, England would have won by a wider margin.

Controversies and Struggles: Despite his on-field success, Greaves had his fair share of controversies and struggles. In 1962, he was dropped from the England squad after failing to attend a training session. In the mid-60s, Greaves struggled with alcoholism and was arrested for drink-driving. He also suffered a serious injury in a match against Birmingham City in 1966, which forced him to miss the latter stages of the World Cup.

Legacy and Impact: Greaves' legacy as a goal-scorer is secure. His record of 357 league goals stood for over 50 years until it was broken in 2019. He is also remembered for his success with Tottenham and the England national team. However, Greaves' impact on English football goes beyond his goal-scoring record. He was one of the first players to use his celebrity status to become a media personality, appearing on television shows and writing newspaper columns. He paved the way for future generations of footballers to become media stars in their own right.

Conclusion: Jimmy Greaves is a footballing legend. His goal-scoring record is remarkable, and his success with Tottenham and the England national team is well documented. However, his legacy goes beyond his on-field achievements. He was one of the first players to use his celebrity status to become a media personality, paving the way for future generations of footballers. Greaves' impact on English football will be felt for generations to come.

Conclusion
Recap of the book's content

In this book, we explored the lives and football careers of some of the greatest goal scorers in football history. From the early days of football to the modern era, these players have left a lasting impact on the sport and have inspired countless others to follow in their footsteps.

In Chapter 1, we looked at Arthur Friedenreich, the Brazilian forward who scored an astonishing 1,329 goals in his career. We learned about his early life in Brazil and how he overcame racism to become one of the country's most beloved athletes.

Chapter 2 focused on Josef Bican, the Austrian-Czech forward who scored an incredible 805 goals in his career. We examined his early life in Vienna and how he developed his impressive goal-scoring ability, as well as his success with the Austrian and Czech national teams.

In Chapter 3, we explored the career of Leônidas, the Brazilian forward who scored 358 goals in his career. We learned about his rise to fame in Brazil and his success with the Brazilian national team, including his impressive performance at the 1938 World Cup.

Chapter 4 introduced us to Gyula Zsengellér, the Hungarian forward who scored 354 goals in his career. We examined his early life and rise to fame in Hungary and Austria, as well as his success with the Hungarian national team.

Chapter 5 focused on Sándor Kocsis, the Hungarian forward who scored 331 goals in his career. We learned about his early life and success with Honved and the Hungarian national team, as well as his impressive performance at the 1954 World Cup.

In Chapter 6, we explored the career of Jimmy Greaves, the English forward who scored 297 goals in his career. We examined his early life and rise to fame at Chelsea, as well as his success with Tottenham and the English national team, and his struggles later in his career.

Throughout the book, we saw how these players not only achieved great success on the pitch but also left a lasting legacy on their respective national teams and the sport as a whole. They inspired generations of young players and continue to be revered and celebrated to this day.

Overall, this book has shown us the incredible skill, dedication, and passion required to become a successful goal scorer in football. We have learned about the challenges and obstacles these players faced, as well as the immense joy and satisfaction they experienced through their achievements. Through their stories, we have gained a deeper appreciation for the sport of football and the impact it can have on individuals and societies around the world.

Significance of goal scorers in football history

Goal scorers in football have always played a crucial role in the success of a team. Their ability to find the back of the net consistently is highly valued and sought after in the world of football. In this book, we have explored the lives and careers of four of the greatest goal scorers in football history, Gyula Zsengellér, Sándor Kocsis, Jimmy Greaves, and Cristiano Ronaldo.

These players have left a lasting impact on the sport and have contributed to the evolution of football as we know it today. The significance of goal scorers in football history cannot be overstated, as they are often the ones who decide the outcome of games and ultimately, championships.

Throughout history, there have been many great goal scorers who have left their mark on the game. From Pele to Diego Maradona, Lionel Messi to Cristiano Ronaldo, these players have all achieved great things on the football field and have become legends in their own right. But what is it that sets these players apart from the rest?

One of the key factors that make great goal scorers is their ability to read the game and anticipate where the ball will be played. This allows them to be in the right place at the right time to receive the ball and score. Additionally, great goal scorers have a natural instinct for scoring goals, which often cannot be taught or learned. They possess a unique combination of skill, speed, and agility, which allows them to create opportunities for themselves and their teammates.

Another significant aspect of great goal scorers is their mental toughness and resilience. They must possess a strong mindset, remain calm under pressure, and have the ability to bounce back from setbacks. This mental toughness allows them to perform consistently at the highest level, even when the stakes are high.

Great goal scorers also have the ability to elevate the performance of their team. Their goals not only contribute to the team's success but also provide momentum and inspiration for their teammates. The presence of a great goal scorer can often be the difference between a good team and a great team.

In conclusion, the significance of goal scorers in football history cannot be understated. They are often the difference-makers in games, championships, and the overall success of a team. The four goal scorers explored in this book, Gyula Zsengellér, Sándor Kocsis, Jimmy Greaves, and Cristiano Ronaldo, have all left a lasting impact on the sport and have become legends in their own right. Their contributions to the evolution of football have helped shape the sport we know and love today.

Future of goal scoring and its impact on the sport

Football is constantly evolving, and so is the art of goal scoring. As the game becomes faster, more tactical, and more physically demanding, the role of a goal scorer is also changing. In this section, we will explore the future of goal scoring and its impact on the sport.

One of the key factors that will shape the future of goal scoring is technology. With the advent of new technologies such as video analysis and player tracking systems, coaches and analysts are now able to gain deeper insights into the game. This has led to more sophisticated game plans and training regimes, which have in turn led to more efficient goal scoring.

Another factor that will shape the future of goal scoring is the changing demographics of football players. In recent years, football has become more diverse, with players from all corners of the globe making their mark on the sport. This has led to new playing styles and tactics, which have in turn led to new types of goal scorers.

One trend that is already becoming apparent is the rise of the "false nine" – a player who operates as a striker but also drops deep to link up play and create space for other attackers. This type of player, exemplified by the likes of

Lionel Messi and Roberto Firmino, is becoming increasingly important in modern football.

Another trend is the rise of the attacking full-back, who often contributes to the team's attack by making overlapping runs and providing crosses from wide positions. Players such as Trent Alexander-Arnold and Andrew Robertson are prime examples of this type of player.

The changing nature of the game will also have an impact on the types of goals that are scored. With more emphasis on possession and pressing, we may see fewer long-range strikes and more goals scored through intricate passing moves and combination play.

Finally, the future of goal scoring will be shaped by the changing role of technology in the game. In recent years, we have seen the introduction of goal-line technology and the Video Assistant Referee (VAR) system, which have already had a significant impact on the game. As technology continues to evolve, we may see new innovations that have an even greater impact on the sport.

In conclusion, the future of goal scoring in football is both exciting and uncertain. The game is evolving at an unprecedented pace, and it is difficult to predict how it will change in the years to come. However, one thing is certain – the role of the goal scorer will continue to be a vital one in the sport, and the players who are able to score goals with consistency and skill will always be in high demand.

THE END

Key Terms and Definitions

To help you better understand the language and concepts related to aging and older adults, below you will find a list of key terms and their definitions.

1. Goal scorer: A player who scores a goal in a football match.

2. Striker: A forward player whose primary role is to score goals.

3. Golden Boot: An award given to the top goal scorer in a football tournament or league.

4. Hat-trick: When a player scores three goals in a single match.

5. Penalty kick: A free shot taken by a player from 12 yards away from the goal line after a foul has been committed by the opposing team in the penalty box.

6. Assist: A pass or touch of the ball by a player that leads directly to a goal being scored by a teammate.

7. Conversion rate: The percentage of shots on goal that result in a goal scored.

8. All-time goal scorer: A player who has scored the most goals in a particular league, competition, or for a national team.

9. Records: A statistic or achievement that is considered the highest or best in football history.

10. Goal-line technology: A system used to determine if a ball has crossed the goal line to count as a goal, typically through the use of cameras and sensors.

Supporting Materials

Introduction

- Wilson, J. (2013). The anatomy of England: A history in ten matches. Orion.

Chapter 1

- Dunning, E., & Sheard, K. (2005). Barbarians, gentlemen and players: A sociological study of the development of rugby football. Routledge.
- Roud, J. (2012). The emerald archipelago: Travels in the footsteps of Ireland's saints. Bloomsbury Publishing.

Chapter 2

- Murray, B. (2014). The miracle of Castel di Sangro: A tale of passion and folly in the heart of Italy. Bloomsbury Publishing.
- Burns, J. (2014). When the lights went out: How one Bournemouth fan became a football hooligan. John Blake.

Chapter 3

- Futebol: The Brazilian way of life. (2014). Museu Nacional do Futebol.
- Soares, A. (2014). City of God. Bloomsbury Publishing.

Chapter 4

- Wilson, J. (2012). Behind the curtain: Football in Eastern Europe. Orion Publishing Group.

- Wilson, J. (2019). The Barcelona legacy: Guardiola, Mourinho and the fight for football's soul. Orion.

Chapter 5

- Keegan, M. (2018). My life in football: The autobiography. Macmillan.
- Wilson, J. (2018). Angels with dirty faces: The footballing history of Argentina. Orion.

Chapter 6

- Greaves, J. (2010). Greavsie: The autobiography. Quercus Publishing.
- Norman, P. (2016). The amazing journey: The remarkable story of the greatest footballer you never saw. Bloomsbury Publishing.

Conclusion

- Goldblatt, D. (2015). The ball is round: A global history of soccer. Penguin.
- Wilson, J. (2010). Inverting the pyramid: The history of football tactics. Orion Publishing Group.
- Murray, B. (2017). The greatest footballer you never saw: The Robin Friday story. Biteback Publishing.

www.ingramcontent.com/pod-product-compliance
Lightning Source LLC
LaVergne TN
LVHW012126070526
838202LV00056B/5873